SOUND SCIENCE

SOUND

SCIENCE

By Melvin L. Alexenberg

Illustrated by Tomie de Paola

Prentice-Hall, Inc., Englewood Cliffs, N.J.

Dedicated to my wonderful wife, Miriam
And to our children Iyrit, Ari, and Ron

Acknowledgement to The Better Reading Foundation, Inc., for permission to reprint problems 6, 7, 10, 11 and 14 which appeared in a similar form as "Science Fun" features by Melvin L. Alexenberg in *Humpty Dumpty's Magazine for Little Children*.

SOUND SCIENCE by Melvin L. Alexenberg © 1968 by Melvin L. Alexenberg All rights reserved. No part of this book may be reproduced in any form by any means, except for the inclusion of brief quotations in a review, without permission in writing from the publisher. Library of Congress Catalog Card Number: 68-15760 Printed in the United States of America Prentice-Hall International, Inc., London Prentice-Hall of Australia, Pty. Ltd., Sydney Prentice-Hall of Canada, Ltd., Toronto Prentice-Hall of India Private Ltd., New Delhi Prentice-Hall of Japan, Inc., Tokyo

Introduction

This book was written to help you find joy in working like a scientist.

A scientist learns how the world works by carefully looking at it.
A scientist checks what he thinks, what he reads, and what other people tell him.
He believes only what he checks by looking at the world itself.

This is a Gloop.

The Gloop will help you find ways to look at the world.
It will help you work like a scientist.

1

Use:

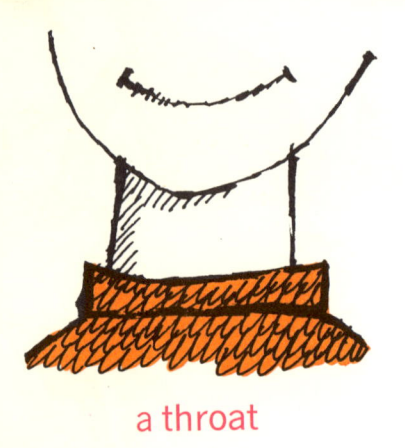

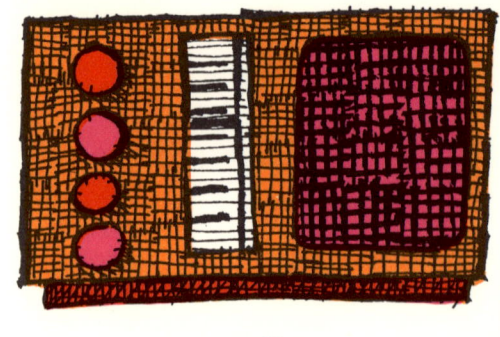

a throat

a radio

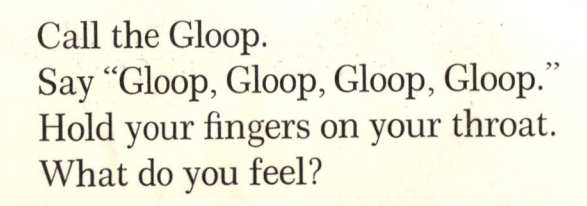

Call the Gloop.
Say "Gloop, Gloop, Gloop, Gloop."
Hold your fingers on your throat.
What do you feel?

Turn on the radio very loud.

Hold your fingers on the part of the radio where
 the sound comes out.
What do you feel?

2

Use:

a skinny rubber band

a fat rubber band

a milk carton

scissors

Cut a big window in one side of the milk carton.
Stretch the skinny rubber band over the carton.
What sound do you hear when you pluck the rubber band?

Look closely at the rubber band while it makes sound.
What do you see?

Try the same thing with the fat rubber band.
Do the skinny and fat rubber bands make the same sound?

3

Use:

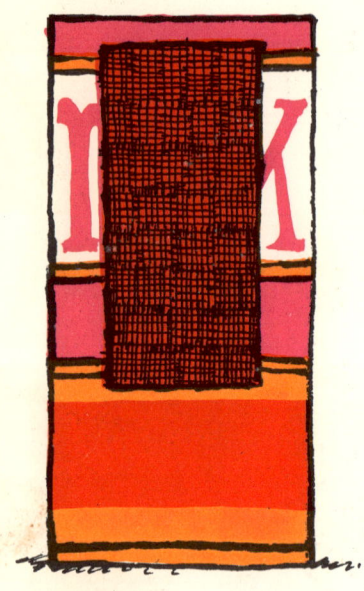

the same milk carton as in 2

a rubber band

a pencil

Stretch the rubber band over the carton.
Push the pencil under the rubber band.

Pluck the rubber band.
What sound do you hear?

Pull the pencil up while you are plucking the rubber band.
Does the sound change as the rubber band is stretched
more and more?

4

Use:

a hacksaw blade

a lump of clay

five books

a table

Put the hacksaw blade on the table so that half of it hangs over the edge of the table.

Put the five books on the part of the hacksaw blade that is on the table.

Stick a lump of clay on the free end of the blade.

Push down on the lump of clay so that the blade moves up and down.

When something moves up and down and up and down,
we say it vibrates.
Watch how fast the blade vibrates.

Pull the blade further out from under the books.
Does the blade vibrate faster?

Push the blade back further under the books.
Does the blade vibrate faster now?

5

Use:

a hacksaw blade

a lump of clay

five books

a table

index cards

a marking pen

Stick the pen to the hacksaw blade with the lump of clay. Make the blade vibrate while half of it is hanging over the edge of the table.

Gently hold an index card against the pen point while the blade is vibrating.

Move the card away from the table so that the pen draws a wavy line on the card.

Pull the blade further out from under the books.

Do the same thing you did before with another index card.

Hold the card that you used this time next to the card you used last time.

Can you use these two cards of wavy lines to tell how fast the blade vibrates?

Does the blade vibrate faster when the free end is long or short?

6

Use:

four soda straws

scissors

Press together one end of each soda straw.
Cut off the corners.
Cut each straw to a different length.

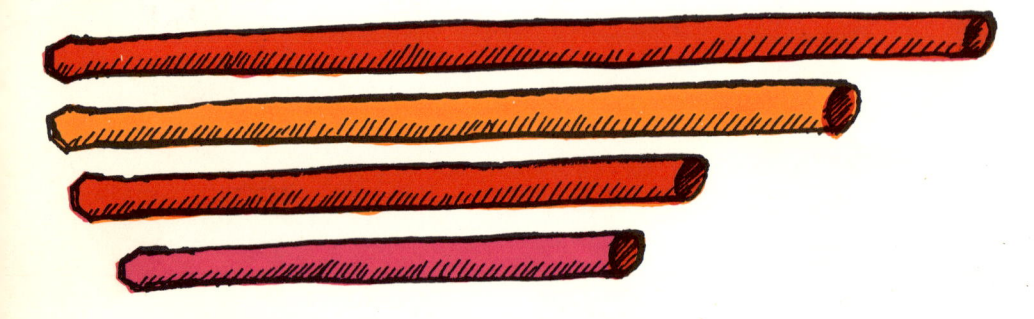

Put the pressed-together end of the longest soda straw into your mouth and blow.
Slowly move the straw further into your mouth until it makes a sound.

Now try blowing through each of the other straws.
Which straw makes the highest sound?
Which straw makes the lowest sound?

7

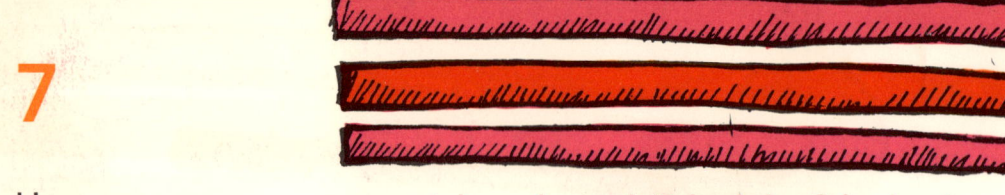

Use:

strips of wood (1 inch by 2 inches)

a ruler

a saw

a spoon

newspaper

tape

Saw the wood into 5 strips.
Cut the first strip 12 inches long.
Cut the second strip 11 inches long, the third, 10 inches, the fourth, 9 inches, and the fifth, 8 inches.

Role up a sheet of newspaper and tape it so that it does not come apart.
Do the same thing with a second sheet of newspaper.
Lay the strips of wood on the paper rolls, longest to shortest.

Tap the strips of wood with the back of the spoon.
What do you hear?
Which strip makes the highest sound?
Which strip makes the lowest sound?

How can you make a sound louder and louder?

8

Use:

5 glasses   a pencil   water

Fill one glass with water.
Pour water into the other four glasses so that it is a different height in each glass.
Line the glasses up in order, from the full one to the one with the least water.

Tap the glasses with the pencil.
What do you hear?
Which glass makes the highest sound?
Which glass makes the lowest sound?
Can you play a song?

9

Use: a spoon

a shoe box   breakfast cereal

Turn the shoe box up-side-down.
Put some breakfast cereal on one end of the shoe box.

Lightly tap the other end of the shoe box with the back of the spoon.
What happens to the cereal?

Hit the box harder and harder.
Does the sound change?
What happens to the cereal as the sound gets louder?

10

Use:

a broomstick   a wristwatch   a friend

Put the broomstick on the floor between you and your friend.
Have your friend hold a wristwatch in his hand.
Can you hear it?

Lift the broomstick up.
Hold one end of it against your ear while your friend holds
   the watch against the other end.

Can you hear the watch now?
Does sound travel better through air or through wood?

11

Use:

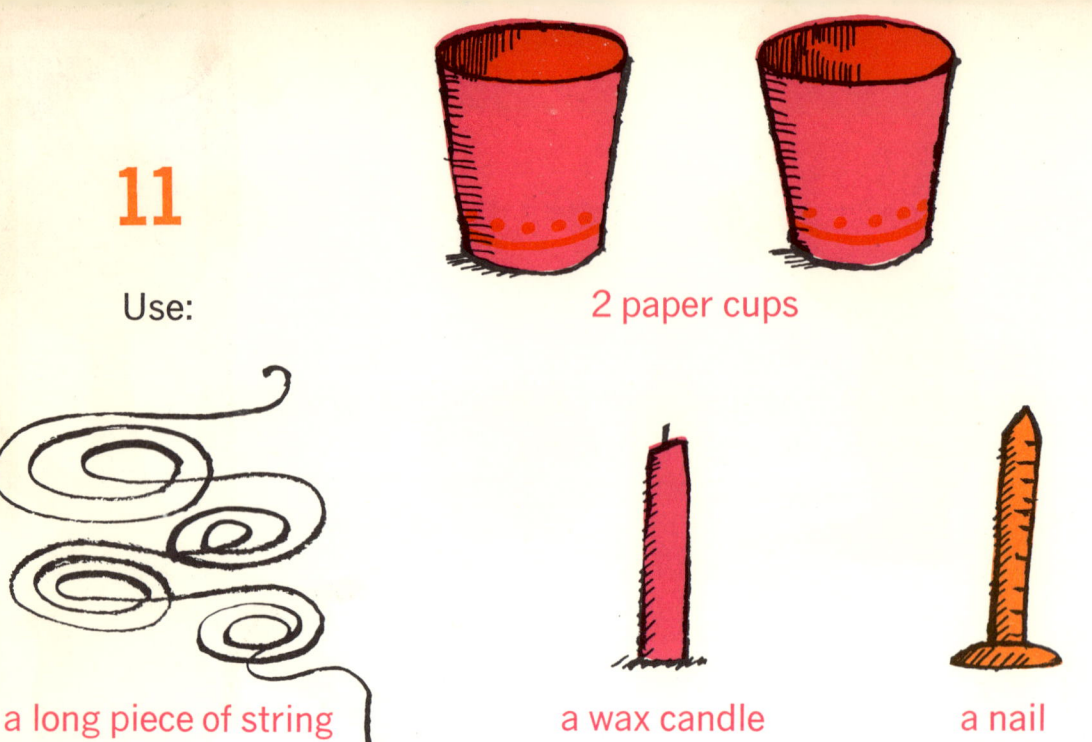

2 paper cups

a long piece of string

a wax candle

a nail

Punch a small hole in the bottom of each paper cup with the nail.
Put the ends of the string through the holes in each cup from the outside.
Tie big knots in the ends of the string so that it cannot pull out of the holes.
Rub the wax candle along the string until all of the string is coated.

Have a friend hold one cup to his ear in the next room
   while you hold the other cup to your mouth.
Pull the string tight.
Then speak softly into the cup.
Ask your friend what he hears.

Now have him talk into the cup.

What do you hear?
Now try talking softly without the paper cup telephone.
Can your friend hear you?

12

Use:

a teaspoon
a soup spoon
a serving spoon

string

a friend

Hold the ends of the string to your ears with your fingers.
Have your friend hang the teaspoon from the string.
Then have him tap the teaspoon with another spoon.
What do you hear?

Do the same thing with the soup spoon.
What do you hear now?

Do the same thing with the serving spoon.
What do you hear?
Which spoon makes the highest sound?
Which spoon makes the lowest sound?

13

Use:

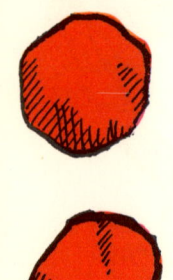

2 rocks **a basin** **water**

Fill the basin with water.
Take one rock in each hand.
Knock them together.
What do you hear?

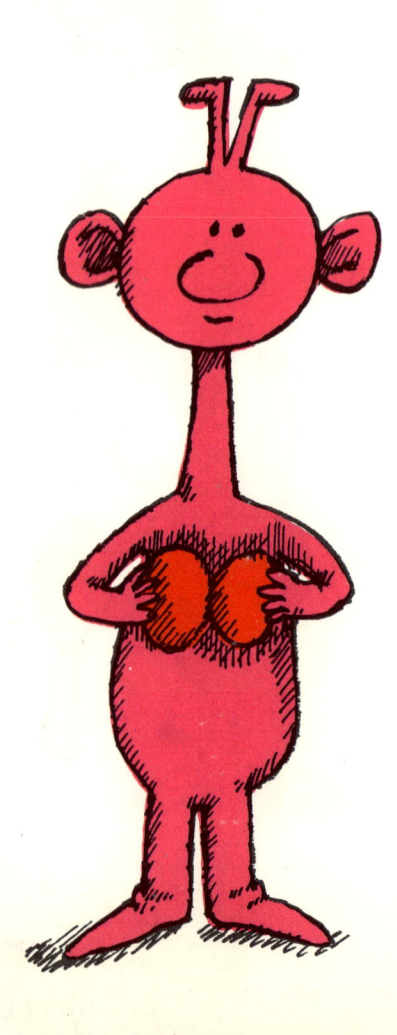

Knock the rocks together under water.
Do you hear anything?
Does sound travel through water?

14

Use:

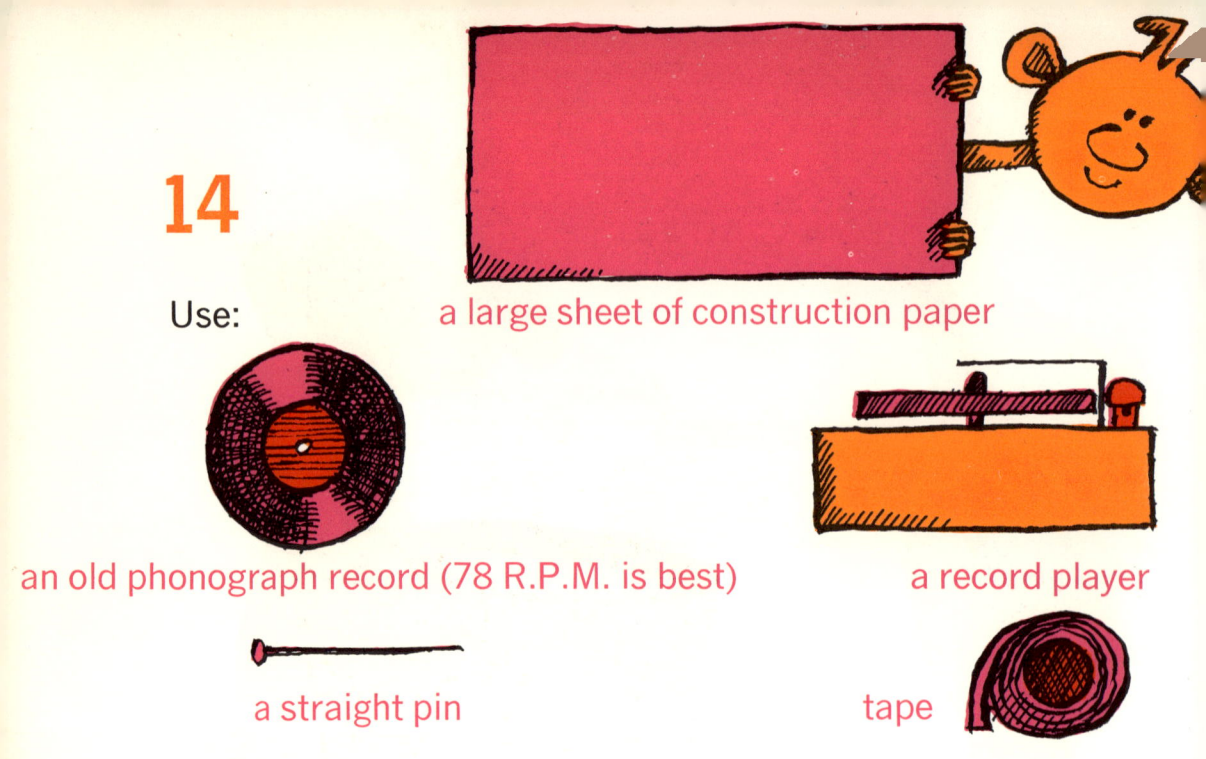

a large sheet of construction paper

an old phonograph record (78 R.P.M. is best)

a record player

a straight pin

tape

Shape the paper into a cone and fold the pointed end.
Tape the cone so that it holds its shape.
Weave the pin through all the layers of paper at the
   small end.

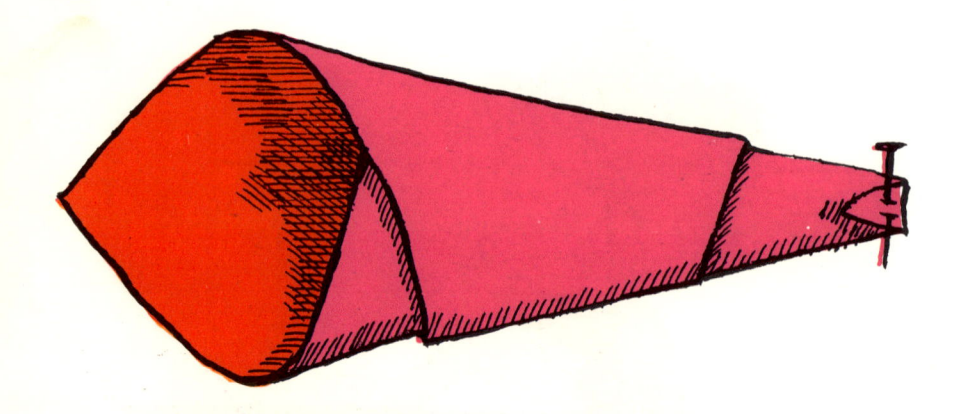

Have the record player turn the record, but do not let the
   needle arm play the record.
Instead, hold the cone and rest the pin lightly in the
   groove of the record.
Have the pin point in the same direction the record turns.
What happens?
What do you feel while you are holding the cone?

Stop the record player and take off the record.
Look closely at its grooves.
If you have a magnifying glass you can see them even
   better.
Are the grooves wavy or straight?
What do the grooves do to the pin in the cone to make
   sound?

15

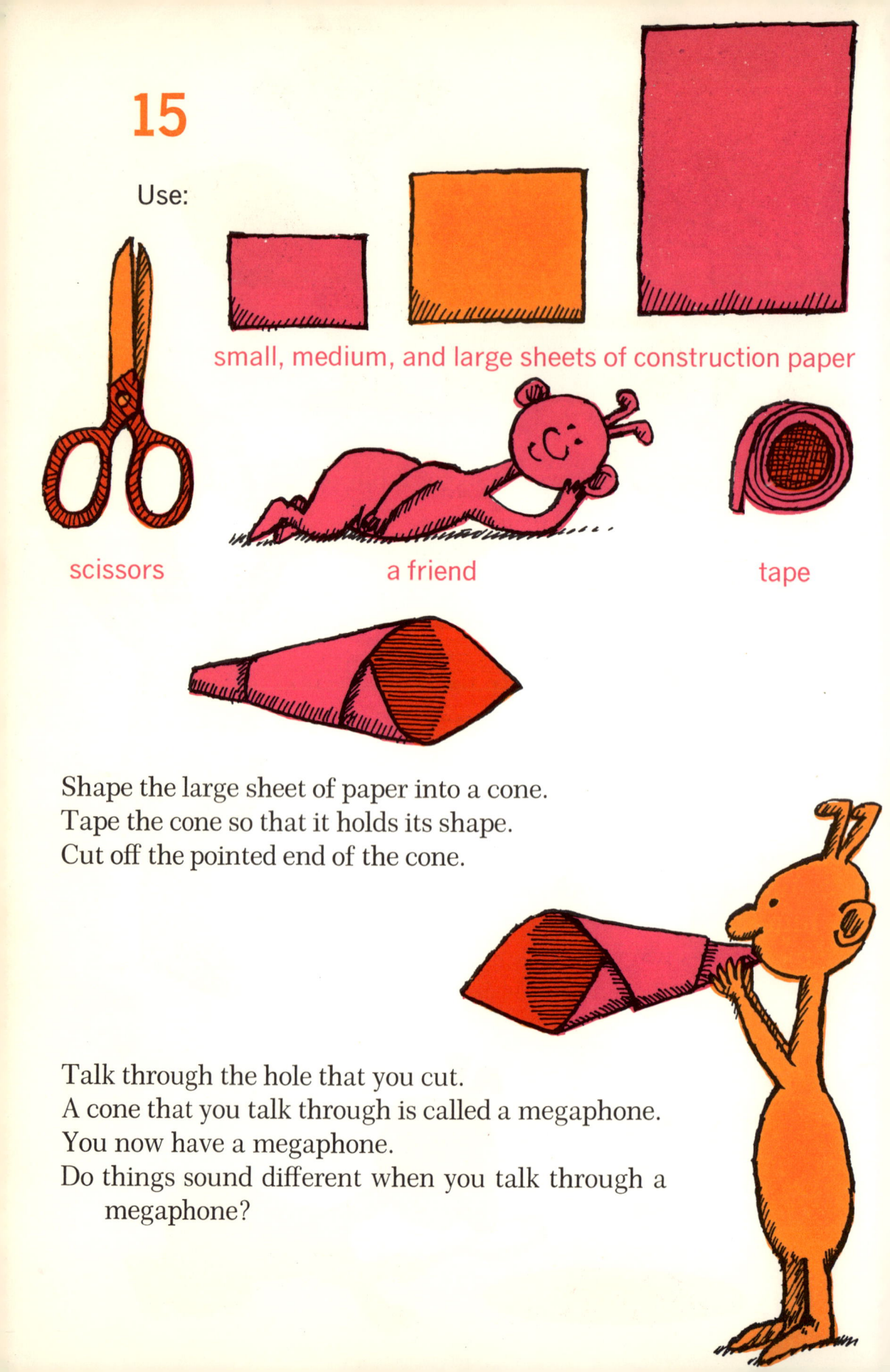

Use:

small, medium, and large sheets of construction paper

scissors   a friend   tape

Shape the large sheet of paper into a cone.
Tape the cone so that it holds its shape.
Cut off the pointed end of the cone.

Talk through the hole that you cut.
A cone that you talk through is called a megaphone.
You now have a megaphone.
Do things sound different when you talk through a megaphone?

Have your friend stand far away from you.
Say something to him without the megaphone.
Then say the same thing just as loud talking through
   the megaphone.
Ask your friend what he heard.

Try the same thing with small and medium size sheets
   of paper.
Do words sound the same through the small and medium
   megaphones as they do through the large megaphone?

16

Use:

a funnel

a wristwatch   a rubber tube   a friend

Rest the wristwatch on a table.
Move away from the table until you cannot hear the wristwatch.

Push one end of the rubber tube into the funnel.
Hold the other end of the rubber tube to your ear.
Hold the funnel over the wristwatch.
Can you hear the wristwatch now?

Hold the funnel against the middle of your friend's chest.
What sound do you hear?
What do you think is making the sound?
Your funnel and tube is like a doctor's stethoscope.
What does a doctor use his stethoscope for?

17

Use:

a chair   a blindfold   a friend

Blindfold your friend while he is sitting on the chair.

Ask him to point to where he thinks you are when you call him.
Stand to the left of your friend and call him.
In what direction does he point?
Stand to the right of your friend and call him.
In what direction does he point now?

Move to different parts of the room and call your friend.
How well can he tell where you are without seeing you?
Are ears good for telling direction?

18

Use:

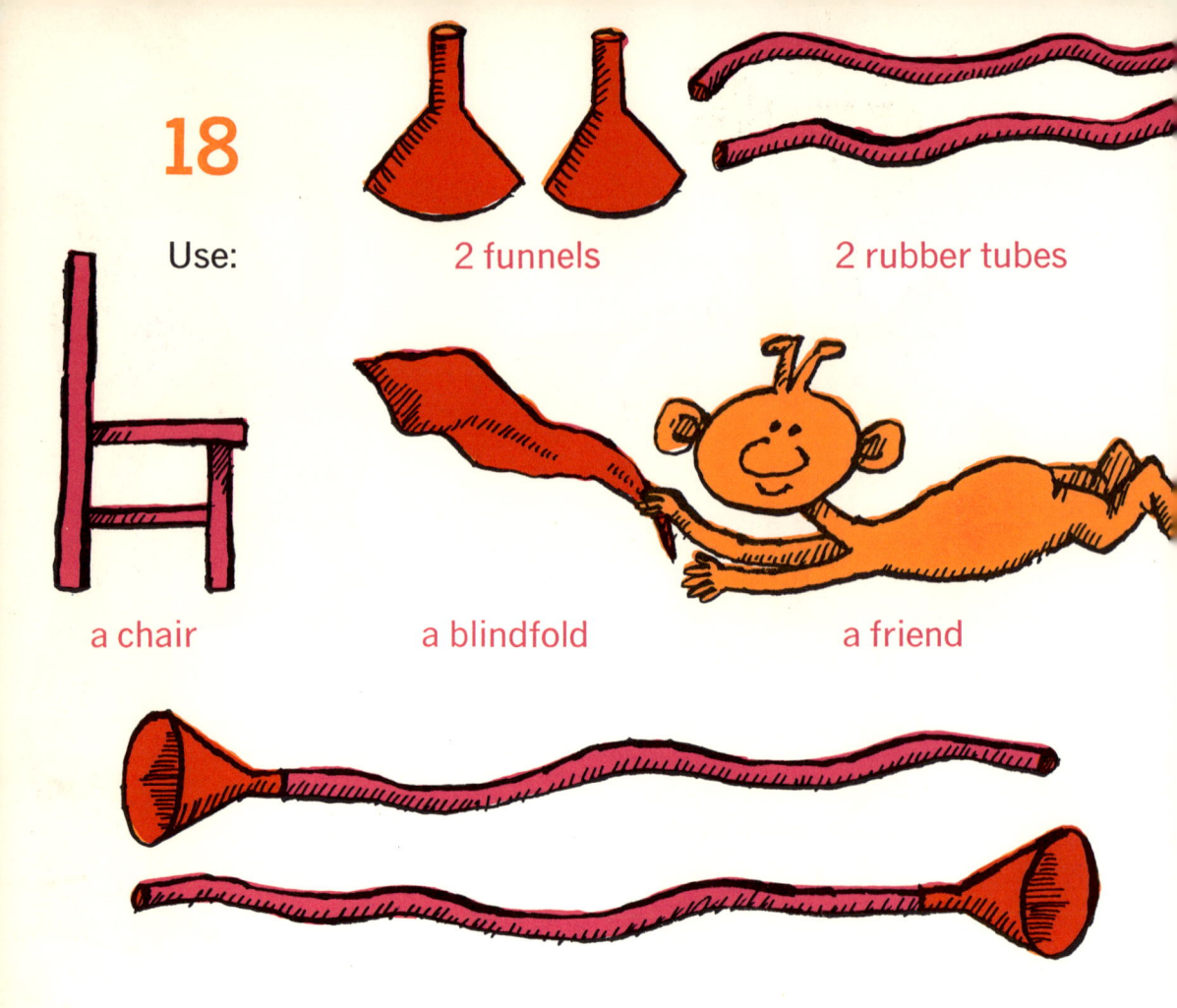

2 funnels

2 rubber tubes

a chair

a blindfold

a friend

Push one end of each rubber tube into each funnel.
Blindfold your friend while he is sitting on the chair.
Ask him to point to where he thinks you are when you call him.
Have him hold the free ends of the rubber tubes to his ears.
Cross the rubber tubes over his head.
Have the tube coming from his right ear end with the funnel on the left side of his head.
Have the tube coming from his left ear end with the funnel on the right side of his head.

Stand to the left of your friend and softly call him.
In what direction does he point?
Stand to the right of your friend and softly call him.

In what direction does he point now?
How do you use your ears to tell direction?

19

Use:

small, medium, and large sheets of construction paper

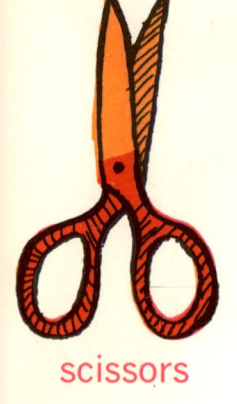

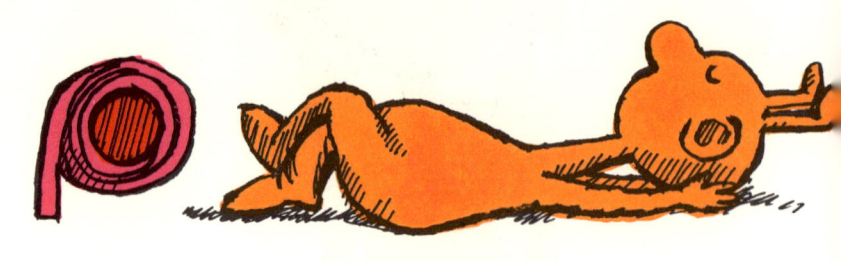

scissors

tape

a friend

Shape the small sheet of paper into a cone.
Tape the cone so that it holds its shape.
Cut off the pointed end of the cone.

Have your friend stand at the other end of the room.
Tell him to keep whispering, "Gloop, Gloop, Gloop, ..."
Cup your hand around your ear.
Does the sound change?

Hold the small end of the cone to your ear.
What do you hear now?

Make medium and large cones and try the same thing.
Take other sheets of paper and make rabbit ears and
  elephant ears.
What do you hear?

A Gloop makes sounds by vibrating his neck.
He can change the pitch of his sounds by making his neck skinny or fat.
Pitch is high or low.

When the Gloop's neck is skinny it vibrates fast.
When his neck is fat it vibrates more slowly.

Does a Gloop whose neck is skinny make a high sound or a low sound?
Find the Gloop that makes the lowest sound.

A Gloop can change the loudness of his sounds by moving his neck further back and forth.
Does a Gloop who moves his neck back and forth very far make a loud sound or a soft sound?
Find the Gloop that makes the softest sound.

A Gloop can send a message to another Gloop by
tapping his foot on the ground.

When do you think a Gloop can hear the tapping best?
Can he hear it better when he is standing up or with
his ear to the ground?

Do you think Gloops can send messages when they are
under water?

There is no air on the moon.
How can Gloops send messages on the moon?

These are Gloops' pets.

Which of the Gloops' pets have ears that catch sound best?

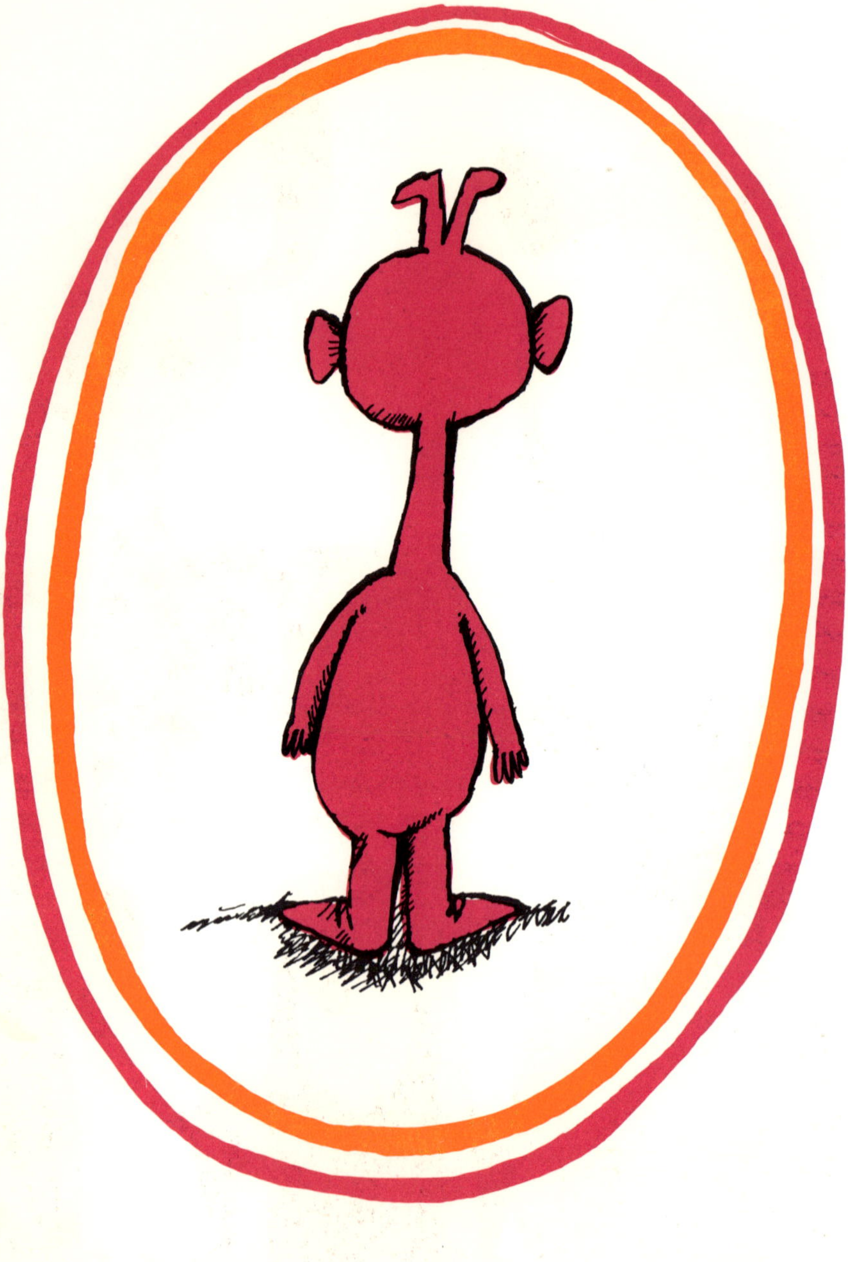

JOHNSON PUBLIC LIBRARY, HACKENSACK, NJ

3 9123 05024942 9

E534.072   230477(W
Alexenberg
Sound science.

DATE DUE